A FAMILIAR TREE

Other books by Jon Stallworthy

*

ROOT AND BRANCH
HAND IN HAND
*(Chatto & Windus with
The Hogarth Press)*
THE APPLE BARREL
(Oxford University Press)

*

BETWEEN THE LINES: W.B. YEATS'S POETRY
IN THE MAKING
VISION AND REVISION IN YEATS'S LAST POEMS
(Oxford University Press)
WILFRED OWEN: A BIOGRAPHY
*(Oxford University Press and
Chatto & Windus)*

JON STALLWORTHY

A Familiar Tree

with drawings by
David Gentleman

OXFORD UNIVERSITY PRESS
NEW YORK

Published jointly by Chatto and Windus
and Oxford University Press

PR
6037
T1615
F3
1978

Library of Congress Cataloging in Publication Data

Stallworthy, Jon.
    A familiar tree.
    I. Title.
    PR6037. T1615F3 1978   821'.9'14   78-16667

    ISBN 0-19-520050-0

© Jon Stallworthy and David Gentleman 1978

Printed in Great Britain

CONTENTS

ACKNOWLEDGEMENTS

So many people have brought tessarae to the making of this mosaic that I cannot hope to acknowledge them all, but I am particularly indebted to my mother and father, Fleur Adcock, Alexander Blok, E. J. Davis, Norman Goodall, Ramsay Howie, Robyn Marsack, Catharine Carver, Carol O'Brien, Peter Stallworthy, and Anne Stevenson.

Acknowledgements are also due to the editors of the following anthologies and magazines in which some of these poems first appeared: *The Draconian, Encounter, A Mandeville Anthology,* 1977, edited by Peter Scupham, *New Poetry 2,* 1976, edited by Patricia Beer and Kevin Crossley-Holland, and *PEN New Poems 1976–77,* 1977, edited by Howard Sergeant. The poems 'Identity Parade' and 'The Almond Tree' appeared in my book *Root and Branch,* 1969.

NICK'S BOOK

The movement of humanity, arising as it does from innumerable arbitrary human wills, is continuous.

To understand the laws of this continuous movement is the aim of history . . . .

The peasants say that a cold wind blows in late spring because the oaks are budding, and really every spring cold winds do blow when the oak is budding. But though I do not know what causes the cold winds to blow when the oak-buds unfold, I cannot agree with the peasants that the unfolding of the oak-buds is the cause of the cold wind, for the force of the wind is beyond the influence of the buds. I see only a coincidence of occurrences such as happens with all the phenomena of life . . . .

To study the laws of history we must completely change the subject of our observation, we must leave aside kings, ministers, and generals, and study the common, infinitesimally small elements by which the masses are moved.

LEO TOLSTOY, *War and Peace*

AT THE CHURCH OF ST JOHN BAPTIST
PRESTON BISSETT
May 1974

Dear John, if a sinner may so
address a saint in his own house,
I come, as others about to go
on a journey have come to these
worn steps, through seven centuries,
to ask a blessing, make their vows,
and look for assent, a sign from your window.

Here they received the names that are
all that remain of them, brown ink
in a parish register,
a shadow on lichened stone:
and among those lifelines, my own.
It draws me outside to the brink
of their graves and it draws me further.

Let me go down to them and learn
what they learnt on their journeys.
And in the looted cavern
of the skull, let me restore
their sight, their broken speech, before
from these worn steps or steps like these
speechless to the speechless I return.

England

MOTHER AND SON
1738

Hush-a-bye baby   on the tree top
I am thy tree and thou
my acorn   an the Lord allow
shall grow to rock acorns and drop

them and see saplings grow in thy shade
Hush-a-bye baby   baby no more
Baby thou went in at the church door
and John thy father   when the parson laid

white hands on thee   said Let his name
be John   *And whatsoever*
Adam called every living creature
that was the name thereof   Thou came'st

hush-a-bye baby   baby no more
John from the font   into the sun
the churchyard where the sexton
was talking to the wind   Thy father bore

thee through the village like a prize calf
greeting the neighbours' God
ha'mercy with a grave nod
a nod for the shout across fields   the laugh

from a thatcher's ladder   So many years
at my goodman's side
stretching my stride
to keep step with the grazier's

and him still a stranger   When the wind blows
the cradle will rock   Sown
in me   grown in me   known
to me always   There   the cock crows

My dearest stranger stirs   and soon the bed
will grumble   shaken to its roots
as he swings out   groping for his boots
He has a calf too   lowing to be fed

OLD JOHN YOUNG JOHN
1744

The day my father stayed in bed
Aunt said   Ann   send the boy out
but I said father said
he would teach me to tickle trout

Not today   nor any day
Aunt said   So I went out and scratched
the pig's back   gave the horses hay
and all the morning watched

them come and go   the other aunts
and neighbour women   all with their
aprons to their eyes   old Chance
the joiner   sniffing the air

and Mister Pearse with his Good Book
At midday mother called me in
Father was lying on his back
with a cloth tied under his chin

Today he came down   in a chest
the uncles carried   set down   let
down   *That which thou sowest
is not quickened   except*

it die   die   halfway to Hell
he stared from darkringed knots   I could
hear him   his hands   as the clods fell
on him   hammering the wood

I was lying above the place
where he caught the freckled trout
when there   far down   was his face
very white   and one hand stretched out

Before I could seize it with mine
the pike   struck   the water boiled

Hush   he is sleeping   Sleep thou   child
and wake a man   his four fields thine

TO THE HONOURABLE MEMBERS
OF THE HOUSE OF COMMONS
1782

Sirs:

    We the undersigned
Freeholders, Farmers, Cottagers
of Preston Bissett, being of one mind,
beg Leave to represent
that those Persons of this Parish
with immemorial Entitlement
to Common Right on Lands some wish
now to inclose, would be deprived thereby
of an inestimable Benefit.
The Beasts they graze on the said Lands supply
their Families with Milk and Meat
in the clenched Belly of the Year,
and furthermore, they now produce
lean Cattle for the Grazier
to fatten and bring at a fair Price
to Market. This we conceive to be
the shortest Path
to Public Plenty and Prosperity,
and we conceive the Aftermath
of the Bill before the House
to be Depopulation of a Village
now filled with vigorous
and hardy Sons of the Tillage,
from whom, and the Inhabitants
of other open Parishes,
the Nation has supplied those Regiments
and Fleets that through the Ages
have been its Strength
and Glory. Driven from the Soil
into the swollen Towns, they must at length

be so enfeebled by their Toil
at Loom and Forge as to debilitate
their Posterity and thence
by slow Degrees obliterate
that Principle of Obedience
to the Laws of God and Man,
which forms the Character of such
as have the Right of Common,
and on which Principle so much
depends the Government
and good Order of the Realm.
These, the Petitioners represent,
will be the Injuries to them
and evil Consequences to the State
of the Inclosure now proposed,
as elsewhere it hath been of late,
and being thus exposed
they pray the House (the Constitutional
Protector of the Poor) to heed
this their Petition that the Bill
may not be suffered to proceed:
and have the Honour to remain
etcetera, Will Richardson,
Josiah Quainton, Henry Payne,
John Stallworthy, Will Orchard, Thomas Dunn.

IN THE NAME OF GOD AMEN

Bowing and scraping   the notary's pen:
This is the last will and testament
of

whom had he the honour to address?
John Stallworthy

and my employment?
Grazier

of what parish?

Pres~
ton Bissett in the County of Buckingham

Name of God   name of grazier
name of parish   Where does a name
come from   what is it worth

in the year
of our Lord one thousand eight hundred
and six

What had I to bequeath?
my soul into the hands of God
and my body to be laid beneath
a decent stone

my goods and chattels?

unto my wife Ann Stallworthy
Also my stock of cattle
and implements of husbandry
And I bequeath unto my sons
John Stallworthy and William
Stallworthy

faith in God's mercy   none
in the justice of men

                    the sum
of twenty pounds apiece

                         my property?
Less to my name in life
than the churchyard holds for me

It is my wish that my said wife
Ann shall succeed me as occupier
of the land I hold and occupy
of Thomas Coke Esquire

once open as the open sky

THE BIRDS O' THE PARISH
circa 1810

Spring come early, spring come late,
When the oak put on its leaves,
The martin and the swallow
Would build beneath the eaves.
But since squire 'closed the common,
Men take the road to town
And thatch where nestlings grew and flew
The wind and rain pull down.

> *Spring come early or late today,*
> *The birds o' the parish are vanisht away.*

Summer come early, summer come late,
The pigeon and the rook
Would lease between the women
Behind the reaping hook.
But since squire 'closed the common
And leasin's called a crime,
Men go to prison for it
And birds are snared in lime.

> *Summer come early or late today,*
> *The birds o' the parish are vanisht away.*

Autumn come early, autumn come late,
The ouzel on the briar
Would sing with those who hewed a log
To feed a cottage fire.
But since squire 'closed the common
And cleared it for the plough,
The poor man must burn cattle dung —
Until he lose his cow.

Autumn come early or late today,
The birds o' the parish are vanisht away.

Winter come early, winter come late,
When icicles grew on the hedge
The sparrow never lacked a crumb
Left on a window ledge.
But since squire 'closed the common,
The poor are starving so
The sparrow on the window ledge
Must stiffen in the snow.

Winter come early or late today,
The birds o' the parish are vanisht away.

WILLIAM
1815

Bells   dinting the afternoon
from Buckingham   Gawcott   and then
the clappers of Bissett   bang   bang
as if Christ were risen again
on a Thursday in June

Happen a great fire   but no smoke
Legged it over the fields   bang   bang
the heart under my smock
to *Victory   Boney to hang*
from an English oak

Tankards passed from The Old Hat
a health to the Duke   one more
and a health to his men   bang   bang
Who dragged the cart out   wood   straw
and the pitch-barrel   who fired that

Tankard empty   tankard full
Brawling for a suck at the bung
Dark   where   what field   nettles my tongue
No quarter   cannon bells   bang   bang
break tower   sky   skull

TO SAMUEL GREATHEED, EVANGELIST,
NEWPORT PAGNELL CHAPEL
1822

Good Master Greatheed,

     do you mind
the boy at Preston Bissett where
you preeched by the In? I am he
lost without light. How do I find
the wickett gate? I pray you gyde
your servant, Sir,

     George Stallworthy

NEWS FROM HOME
1831

My nephew,
      Have our troubles come
to your godly ears? Red sky at night
a rick alight, and at Wycomb
last month the bloodiest fight
I ever saw. Came shouts at dawn,
uproar outside the inn, the sound
of feet and a rallying horn.
It was a band of labourers bound
on violent business, so their staves
and sledgehammers declared. One called
my name: he with the horn, Ned Graves,
your school-fellow. 'We're one and all!'
said he. I fell in step with him,
asking what brought him there. 'A purse
and belly with nothing in them.'
I prayed him keep the peace lest worse
befall. At which he blew his horn.
We had come to the edge of town
and a mill, whose gates were soon sawn
from their hinges. Someone threw down
vitriol and many were burned
as they burst in. The new machines
were sledgehammered till no cog turned
another. There were violent scenes
at other mills. A cleric read
the Riot Act. 'Be off and claim
your thirty pieces!' shouted Ned.
And then the soldiers came.

      Today at Aylesbury I heard
false witness from a man of God.

25

God repay him. It went hard
with Ned. Transported — dreadful word —
for seven years. Because he had
no work, transported seven years.
Because his children cried for bread
at night, transported seven years.
Because he blew a horn, because
a vicar valued the truth less
than tithes, transported seven years.
How, if the shepherd so transgress,
shall sheep not stray? Are there not rams
caught in our thickets, and can you
not set them free? Are heathen lambs
more hungry than our own? Nephew,
your fathers' flocks are calling. Shall
they call in vain?

                John Stallworthy

PATCHWORK
1833

A house without a man
a pod without a pea
William gone   under the ground
George going   over the sea
Come little needle   you
and I have work to do

Grey silk   for the village
William's wedding vest
and this for God's Acre
my cotton Sunday-best
with the Michaelmas daisies
He always liked these

For Claydon Brook   a ribbon
Lenborough Wood   sateen
remnants of chintz and twill
the crowded fields between
and from this pair of sleeves
a border of oak leaves

Though seas be heaped between us
my son shall sleep at home
and when he takes a bride
may she find here with him
on this familiar ground
what William and I found

THE *TUSCAN*
16 October 1833

My dear Uncle,
                    Lying tonight
at Gravesend, joyful augury
of our journey's end, I write
from a full heart.
    As we came aboard,
a cloud inland outran the rest
unfurling, as it swirled toward
us, wings that darkened the bright West,
shadowed the shore and estuary.
Above the listening ship it broke
and every mast became a tree
again, budded with birds. They spoke
to me shrilly of home, their mud
nests under your eaves, and your voice
calling me. But the voice of God
was calling them South. I rejoice
to have heard His summons. May His cloud
of witnesses speak in the Spring
to you: of heathen fields well ploughed,
well planted and worth harvesting
as any in Preston Bissett.
    Although you cannot approve
or bless my choice, do not forget
one who remembers you with love,

        Your nephew George

The Marquesas

Pages from a Journal

THE DEPARTURE
17 October 1833

From Gravesend on the morning tide.
God forgive me that I wrote
'a joyful augury', in my pride
forgetting poor Ned Graves, afloat
in irons. On deck, thinking of him
between decks, watched the harbour sink
beneath our wake and sang a hymn
to mend my spirits.

THE ARRIVAL
22 March 1834

Only the wind was up before me
and the man at the wheel, who said,
'Listen, her timbers talk in their sleep,
the masts sing a new song. When she
smells land, you can give her her head.'
Darkness was upon the face of the deep.

The Spirit of God moved upon the face
of the waters. And God said,
Let there be light: and there was light.
And God said, Let the dry land
appear: and it was so. Ahead,
not a cloud, but a mountain, foliage, sand,

and canoes putting out. Like birds
of paradise their plumes, the flash
of their wings as they crossed
the bay. Bird-men chanting the words
of Satan! Tattooed on their flesh
the mark of Cain! Are these my people? Christ

with his blood shall wash their sins away.
And what to say of that shoal
of girls, gambolling in their wake,
who climbed aboard by the bob-stay?
Such bodies, unveiled, put the soul
in peril! Dear God, see how my hands shake —

as the ship has shaken since.
Lascivious dances on the upper
deck! Foul songs to a fiddle-stick
that led our hymns! Intemperance —
and worse! Some, that last Sunday took
the sacrament, coupling in the scuppers!

THE BEGINNING
16 April 1834

The Word was God. God: *Atua*.
Atua in my mouth. Mouth: *Fafa*.
Lord, though they mock me, yea, though they
mock Thy Word; though warriors say:
How shall a man who eats his God
rebuke a man who thinks it good
to eat his enemy? they yet
shall turn from murder, take, eat
bread from a fire their idols fed.

THE CONTEST
10 August 1834

He with his puppet, I with my *Testament*
met in the *marae,* under a breadfruit tree,
when all the chiefs and warriors were present.

He cried out: '*Te-erui* made the islands. He
made *Tahuata.*'
                    I: 'Not so. There iṣ
but one God, maker of Heaven and Earth.
He made *Tahuata* and it is His.'

He: '*Te-erui* the first man.'
                    I: 'Who gave birth
to *Te-erui*?'
            He: '*O Te-tareva.*'
I: 'Whence came *Te-tareva*?'
                    He: '*Avaiki,*
under all things. He climbed up and over
Tahuata.'
            I: 'Then it was here when he
climbed up?'
            He: 'Without doubt.'
                              Into my hands,
O Lord, did'st thou deliver the Priest of Baal.

I: 'How did *Te-erui* make the land
if his progenitor found hill and vale
established before his birth?'
                    To this he gave
no answer. And addressing then the multitude,
I spoke of God, the Creation, Adam and Eve,
and their transgression redeemed by our Lord's blood.
Lord, let thy Sower's seed fall on good ground. Amen.

THE TRIALS
12 March 1837

Light is come amongst them, but they
love darkness rather than light.
Five canoes I saw yesterday
put to sea southward and last night,
in a pit lined with stones, a fire
was lit, I thought, to guide them home.
Tonight, over a red sea, four
returned like moths to their tall flame
and conches bellowing round
the bay. I took my evening walk
that way, and in the firelight found
the warriors at such butcher's work
as froze my blood and now my ink.

18 March 1837

The Rodgersons will not stay:
'the island being unfit', they think,
'for civilized females'. Since they
found hideous fruit in the fork
of a tree, she has not slept. They go
next week. And I? *Yea, though I walk*
through the valley of the shadow
of death, I will fear no evil:
rather, will I rejoice
with you to guide me, Lord, and fill
my silence with an English voice.

23 August 1844

How long must these false shepherds, Lord,
seduce your flock before they feel
your rod? Another teacher lured
from school by practices most foul,
lies, popish lies! The Frenchman buys
souls with a gourd of holy water,
selling his own soul for the eyes
of Chief Totete's daughter.

18 December 1847
At Falealili. Marriage with Miss Darling

Old sobersides, is there
no more to say than that?
No praise for my bonnet,
no lament for your hat
blown overboard? Come, bless
the Lord for happiness

that your holy wooing
had not prepared me for.
Admit that your mother,
at least, would not deplore
the pleasure that we found
on her 'familiar ground'!

27 January 1855

My fever by God's grace abating, I
cut coffins until noon — the smallest one
from my own flesh for my own flesh — while my
dear partner sewed and Apu dug the grave
(breaking a mattock blade). When all was done,
we buried them in the breadfruit grove.
Eight in the earth and seven gathered round
to hear the words of comfort, which a flock
of clamorous parakeets all but drowned.
Blessed are the dead which die in the Lord.

Order from home:—

1   pickaxe
1   mattock
1   stonecutter's chisel
2   balls whipcord
4   hatchets
12 yds linen
ditto lint
rose cuttings
seeds — geranium, hollyhock,
      thyme, parsley, tarragon, rosemary, mint

5 April 1859

He has spoken in thunder, He has stretched forth
His rod, and the wind and the waters rose
and the sun went down on His wrath.
Rain hissed along the thatch like arrows,
or what we took for rain until, at dawn,
we tasted salt and saw the sea. Our boat
it seemed must founder, or be torn
from its moorings and dashed to pieces. But
we prayed and, Faith prevailing, we forbore
to violate the Day ordained for Rest
by hauling it to safety on the shore.
All day the travail of the deep increased
as though the Last Trump should bring forth its dead.
Night fell, but not the wind and not the tide,
which roaring marched inland. The natives fled
to higher ground but nowhere could they hide
from His chastisement. As my household knelt
in prayer, the roof was blown off and we felt
beneath us three such shocks it seemed the tap-
root of the land must snap.
Out of the depths have I cried unto thee,
O Lord. Lord, hear my voice. And He gave ear,
restraining the salt wind, bidding the sea
retire. Released from the burden of fear,
my wife and children on the wet ground slept.
And I went forth to view His vengeance who
is just and merciful. The wan moon crept
from a cloud, revealing no prospect I knew
but a spectacle awful and sublime.
Taboo grove, the huts of the heathen, where
were they? All levelled: every palm tree plume

abased, every plantain root in the air,
the yam crop vanished down the ocean's throat,
our chapel and the Papist's beaten flat,
but praise God! eighty yards inland, our boat
unscarred as the Ark upon Ararat.

2 May 1859

It is God's will. Again He stretches forth
His rod, and caterpillars now complete
His punishment of a dissolute
people: *they covered the face of the whole earth,*
so that the land was darkened; and they did eat
every herb of the land, and all the fruit
of the trees which the hail had left: and there
remained not any green thing in the trees,
or in the herbs of the field, through all the land
of Egypt.
               Obscene maggot, do you dare
march even to my desk, my journal? These
have no crops for you. The pen in my hand
ploughs a poor furrow — but see — it can fill
your belly forever! God forgive me,
I have slain the agent of His will.

6 November 1859

Notes for the graveside: Sower and seed.
Our brother Apu the good ground
giving roots room, stalk strength, to bear
the swelling grain. Flour. Bread to feed
a famished people. That good ground,
harrowed, yet shall bear
His fruit an hundredfold. And I
see Apu throned in glory over us,
affirming his Master's promise
of lasting harvest. 'Let me die
the death of the righteous,
and let my last end be like his.'

THE RETURN
7 November 1859

His pen — his journal — but
the living hand that should
unite them by lamplight —
stilled under a shroud
the patchwork map of home
his mother stitched for him.

The hand that was our shield
struck down by a greater!
Husband, I cannot kneel
to praise the Creator
who with a stroke has felled
His shepherd and His fold.

The bonnet trimmed with lace
while you wrote in this book
has gone to the closet
from which, tonight, I took
the old black bonnet
with all our sorrows on it.

It and I tomorrow
and your — orphans — must they
be called — shall follow you,
but not to hear you say
'I name this child'. He cries
for me. I kiss your eyes.

16 December 1859

My dear husband, it is
finished. We are afloat
and bound for Gravesend. Once
in this cabin you wrote
your journal with the pen
I now take up again

to tell you how we left.
The brethren, visibly
affected, gave us each
a garland on the quay,
gathered in that high glade
where my two loves are laid.

You sank into the earth,
and then into the sea.
Winged spirit, protect us!
Tonight, keep watch with me
and cool the fevered limbs
of our distempered lambs.

17 December
Louisa cannot swallow.

18 December
Daybreak — Louisa gone.

20 December
At Rarotonga — laid
Sarah by William. John
gave, at the last, a cry —
'Why do you plant them?' Why

New Zealand

MOTHER AND SON
1872

Dear Johnny,
          I had such
a dream, nodding last night
over your father's charts.
We were at sea — in sight
of a mountain, foliage, sand —
you and I, hand in hand,

watching the sun come up
behind Tahuata.
To starboard, a canoe
struck sparks from the water.
In the bows — can you guess?
Arms semaphoring — yes,

your father! The canoe
came on. Paddles were shipped.
His hands reached up to me,
but in my haste I slipped
down through the green crevasse,
which closed above me as

I woke — without husband
or son, my bed as cold
as the bed of the sea.
But soon, hearing swifts scold
their young under the eaves,
I thought: they too will leave

in the wake of the sun —
my son — and with the Spring,
please God, all will return.
God in his mercy bring
my sailor — and bring them —
home to
　　　　your loving M.

THE ARRIVAL
1873

My dear Mother,
                              Riding a kauri spar
I came to the New World, and ride today
kauris downriver to the hungry saw —
'What is a kauri?' I can hear you say.

   A thousand years ago it was a seed
that sprung a root the land took to its heart,
raised to a sapling slender as a reed.
Before the land existed on a chart,
its dark veins fed the dark veins of the tree
and swelled the lengthening grain, the branching crown
that lifted century by century,
as ferns and tree-ferns rose and rotted down.
In a cathedral nave not made with hands
but by the living God it took its place
and, sweetening the air with resin, stands
till the cross-cut gnaws at its base.
The pillar falls, its crown falls to the axe,
and the great trunk travels 'the rolling road'
with block and tackle and timber-jacks
to where the bullock teams take up the load
and, some miles on, the torrent that in spring
will bring it to my feet.
                              The creek in spate
drives the wild timber, bucking, rearing,
down to the river where we pikemen wait
to herd them into rafts. Then the slow miles —
bell-bird and mouth-organ telling the hours —
to Sawdust City and its howling mills.
The pistons slog. The Circular devours
the past to build the future, plank by plank.

51

It is a grand life, Mother. Putting half
my shilling a day in the Temperance Bank,
I shall sit by your fireside soon enough —
with a full wallet and a fob-watch on!

This piece of kauri gum brings the compressed
light of a thousand years
                                                and my love
                                                            John

RETURN TO SENDER. ADDRESSEE DECEASED.

A PROPOSAL
1874

Dear Marion,
           I was never more
in earnest in my life
than when on the North Shore
I asked you to be my wife.
And should my prospects appear less
than your father would wish,
I have had some success
and what could not accomplish
if you would put your hand in mine —
as I have mine in His
who made the sun and moon,
the earth and all that therein is?
He will not fail me, Marion.
Say yes to Him, say yes to
                    John

A PRAYER
1908

Dear God,
      Forgive me that at first,
despairing, I said 'Why
hast Thou forsaken me?' and cursed
the day that I was born. Thirty
years' labour turned to bitter smoke —
print-shop and paper store!
But later, when the morning broke
through rafters, wall, and floor,
the voice of Job at my ear said:
'The Lord gave, and the Lord
hath taken away; blessed
be the name of the Lord.'
Grant me strength and a mortgage, Lord,
and new works to proclaim
the fiery essence of Thy Word,
the glory of Thy name.

AN EXPOSTULATION
1911

Father,
      Your accusations I
emphatically deny.
Was I so 'self-obsessed',
so 'blinded with self-interest':—

   When leaving school at eleven
I worked without being driven
at your machines all day?

   When at thirteen I put away
my cricket bat and football boots
and all boyish pursuits
to be your ledger clerk?

   When every morning in the dark
I saddled up and rode the rounds
of Dargaville? £2
a week I saved the till
delivering *The Wairoa Bell*,
and not a thumbworn threepenny bit
did I receive for it
till I was 21.

   When since, with never a 'well done'
for years of unpaid overtime,
I slaved, helping you climb
the treacherous ascent
from hustings into Parliament?

When I insured the works and drew
£600 for you
but asked not a penny
for everything the fire cost me?

  Anyone reading your letter
would think me little better
than a thief. You claim
I banked your money in my name.
What are the facts? When you were called
to higher things, were all
the wages paid from Heaven?
Acting on your instructions then
I banked what came in, and paid out —
as you for years had not —
all that was due, except
to me. For 6 years I have kept
my peace, rashly believing your
best interests mine. No more.
Either you let me buy
the firm for a fair price, or I —
and half your business — leave in May.
The choice is yours.

                    A J

WITH A COPY OF
EARLY NORTHERN WAIROA
1916

My dear George,
              Providence has crowned
my labours in a new sphere with success.
My book is written and printed and bound.
May this first copy from the (Albion) press
divert and comfort you, calling to mind
those others far from Home who in their day
fashioned the Dominion you defend.
God defend you, body and soul (they say
the French are slaves to alcohol and worse).
    We here are fighting the good fight as well.
Last month the Liquor Trade suffered a reverse,
when our petition cost the Creek hotel
its licence for disorder. This shall be
a country fit for heroes (when the Hun
is crushed) and for their children, sober, free,
serving the Lord with gladness. My dear son,
the Lord lift up the light of his countenance
upon you and give you peace now and for
evermore.
           Dad

A COUPLE OF FIELD POSTCARDS
1917

Dear Dad,
        Ta for the book.
I read it, and it came
in handy when a shell took
our Woodbines. Now your name
is on everyone's lips!
Providence, you could say
atoning for its lapse!
Don't worry. From today,
lying as low as
a tick in the wool, I'll
roll my own Wairoas
and Smile, Smile, Smile.
                  G.

1919

Dear Dad,
        Those who subscribed
to your public fountain
may never have imbibed
a better drink than rain.
I do not mind them thinking
'Water's the best beverage',
but had I not been drinking
whisky on Vimy Ridge,
body and soul would not
today keep company.
So I'll be voting 'wet'
in the election.
                  G.

CONGRATULATIONS
1932

Good on you, Doctor John!
To think I'd live to see
the nephew that rode on
my shoulders an M.D.
I hear you want to go
to London and folk say
'What for?' I know and so
would they, by God, if they
had fought through France — towards
the Conquering Heroes' quay-
side welcome, the fine words,
the stony section.
                    G.

THE RETURN
1934

Rounding the Horn, such seas!
and at the edge of sight
always an iceberg crest.
Strapped in my bunk at night
feeling the ship drop
too far and fast to stop,

I waited for the blow,
the torn plates spouting, time
after time. But then
shuddering she would climb
out from under the wave
pouring into her grave.

If she was his patient,
my dear ship's doctor said,
he would a hundred times
have given her up for dead,
but still her pulses beat
strongly under our feet.

And entering the Bay
of Biscay, as the gale
blew out, we found a bird
exhausted on the rail —
like Noah's dove — swallow
or swift, I do not know.

Its tail a tattered flag
drooped at the stern, and yet
by that magnetic beak

the helmsman could have set
his course for Home — to which,
perhaps, it was as much

a stranger as were we.
The trumpet of the spring
was calling him, and when
he followed it, something
turned over in me, wild
and joyful, like a child.

England

HOME THOUGHTS FROM ABROAD
3 September 1939

Dear Dad,
         The 9 o'clock news says 'War',
and whatever that means, it means that we're
not to see Christmas in NZ. Britain
will need — if her future is written
in flames over Warsaw — more doctors soon
than all her drawling Fortnum & Mason
heirs to brass plates in the shires. And how
shall our barbarian be schooled now?

HOME THOUGHTS FROM ABROAD
1955

        'The finest blades in Rome',
he told my father that first morning, 'come
from this forge. Give me a lump of your
Etruscan, Roman, Syracusan ore
and in ten years I'll have a sword for you
fit for the Emperor's side.' Scuffing a new
sandal in father's shadow, I worried
that riddle round my head — and have carried
it since like a burr. He said: 'I need not tell
you, sir, there's more than good metal
to a good sword.' I was to learn how much.

The firing, first:
        'If a cohort can march
thirty miles in battle-order — full pack
and tools — you can walk to the baths and back
like men, not slaves.' 'Centurion, how many
miles did you march in Germany?'
If some doubted his rank, none could deny
his scars: the blue grave on his thigh
of splinters from a Parthian lance; his arms
notched with a tally of battles, night alarms,
ambushes — 'road, river, *our* line, *their* line'
sketched in the schoolyard sand. The Cisalpine
frontier burned at our backs, and its ash fell
on Rome that year and the next year as well;
ash freighting every wind, blighting one roof
in ten. The mothers of my friends wore grief
and Gaius, Marcus, and Marcellus missed
a week of school. Whenever the rest
played Romans and Barbarians, those three
would not draw lots for Spartacus and Pompey,

66

Caesar and Vercingetorix
                    The years
brought back from their resonant frontiers
proconsular heroes, whose names were cut
across the blackened benches where we sat
to hear them speak of Rome . . . of her galleys
and viaducts as the earth's arteries
flowing with grain and metal . . . and of work
to be done in the eagles' endless wake.

From fire to anvil:
                    over an iron knee
we learnt the rule of law. Justice decreed
three hammer blows for bad hexameters,
four for disrespect to gods or ancestors,
five for disloyalty, six for deceit,
and one for flinching when the hammer beat.

From fire to anvil, anvil to water —
breaking its skin each morning in winter
to steel our own against the furious
skies of the frontiers awaiting us.
The frontiers of the body we pushed back,
wrestling, mapped them on the running track,
until we ruled ourselves; until, after
ten years, we were the men our fathers were.
But fired, forged, tempered, and tested, when we looked
for eagles to follow, all were plucked
naked by northern winds.
                    Today my state,
though not proconsular, is fortunate
enough. For National Servicemen with time
to kill, better the White Man's Grave than tame
parades beside the Rhine or 'bull' at home.
We do no good here and we do no harm,

as they did both, whose colours still at dawn
we hoist above the palms, at dusk haul down.
Come 'Independence', those will be laid up,
and the last legionaries played to their ship
by Hausa bugles, Ibo fifes. When quit
of us, they'll come to blows, but now all's quiet
on the Western Frontier.
                                        Tomorrow,
I'm Duty Officer; tonight, must borrow
some Regular's sword for my Sam Browne.
You wonder what the sword's for? Pulling down
thunderbox lids that nobody cleans
in the Royal West African Frontier Force latrines.

IDENTITY PARADE
before the shaving mirror
1959

So, you have noticed: I am not
the man he was — the big-shot

captain of the First XV.
His jersey, cramped in polythene,

glows in my cupboard but is half
my size. Your photograph

shows someone else of the same name
confident before the big game.

He knows who he is and where he
is heading, but wouldn't know me

from 22925028,
the subaltern in a slouch hat.

His company in single file
threaded on a compass needle

stitch the map. He leads. He knows
at each river-bank the shallows

from the stream. If, as you tell
me, once I knew him well

we grew apart many years back.
These mornings at the eight o'clock

identity parade I am
a stranger to myself; the sum

of many strangers, who today —
since I have lost their way —

reproach me to my face. You should
get up and go shouts the blood

in my wrist — is it theirs or mine?
Without touchline or gridline

where should I go? Towards that still
mythical stranger whose stare will

appraise — commend or deride —
my choice. I can decide. Decide.

The Almond Tree
Jonathan: 1960

I

All the way to the hospital
the lights were green as peppermints.
Trees of black iron broke into leaf
ahead of me, as if
I were the lucky prince
in an enchanted wood
summoning summer with my whistle,
banishing winter with a nod.

Swung by the road from bend to bend,
I was aware that blood was running
down through the delta of my wrist
and under arches
of bright bone. Centuries,
continents it had crossed;
from an undisclosed beginning
spiralling to an unmapped end.

II

Crossing (at sixty) Magdalen Bridge
Let it be a son, a son, said
the man in the driving mirror,
Let it be a son. The tower
held up its hand: the college
bells shook their blessing on his head.

III

I parked in an almond's
shadow blossom, for the tree
was waving, waving me
upstairs with a child's hands.

71

IV

Up
the spinal stair
and at the top
along
a bone-white corridor
the blood tide swung
me swung me to a room
whose walls shuddered
with the shuddering womb.
Under the sheet
wave after wave, wave
after wave beat
on the bone coast, bringing
ashore — whom?
                              New-
minted, my bright farthing!
Coined by our love, stamped with
our images, how you
enrich us! Both
you make one. Welcome
to your white sheet,
my best poem!

V

At seven-thirty
the visitors' bell
scissored the calm
of the corridors.
The doctor walked with me
to the slicing doors.
His hand upon my arm,
his voice — *I have to tell
you* — set another bell

beating in my head:
your son is a mongol
the doctor said.

VI

How easily the word went in —
clean as a bullet
leaving no mark on the skin,
stopping the heart within it.

This was my first death.
The '*I*' ascending on a slow
last thermal breath
studied the man below

as a pilot treading air might
the buckled shell of his plane —
boot, glove, and helmet
feeling no pain

from the snapped wires' radiant ends.
Looking down from a thousand feet
I held four walls in the lens
of an eye; wall, window, the street

a torrent of windscreens, my own
car under its almond tree,
and the almond waving me down.
I wrestled against gravity,

but light was melting and the gulf
cracked open. Unfamiliar
the body of my late self
I carried to the car.

VII

The hospital — its heavy freight
lashed down ship-shape ward over ward —
steamed into night with some on board
soon to be lost if the desperate

charts were known. Others would come
altered to land or find the land
altered. At their voyage's end
some would be added to, some

diminished. In a numbered cot
my son sailed from me; never to come
ashore into my kingdom
speaking my language. Better not

look that way. The almond tree
was beautiful in labour. Blood-
dark, quickening, bud after bud
split, flower after flower shook free.

On the darkening wind a pale
face floated. Out of reach. Only when
the buds, all the buds, were broken
would the tree be in full sail.

In labour the tree was becoming
itself. I, too, rooted in earth
and ringed by darkness, from the death
of myself saw myself blossoming,

wrenched from the caul of my thirty
years' growing, fathered by my son,
unkindly in a kind season
by love shattered and set free.

74

ONE FOR THE ROAD
May 1974

Dear Nick,
      I write this letter now
because by the time you can read
you will have forgotten how
with a new map, an old book,
and a following wind we took
the Tingewick-Preston Bissett road.
The wind had dismasted an oak — its bough

breaching the hedge its saplings thickened —
and the swifts were skiing for joy
over clouds at their journey's end:
the village to whose bright square
we returned, who had last been there
in the lurching veins of a boy
bound for the *Tuscan* lying at Gravesend.

No trace in the house of the saint
of George, his servant. But I found
in God's Acre my Red Devilment
free-falling from *James Stallworthy*
Died . . . 1773
aged 3 years. You were 3.
         The ground
split, showing the vertiginous descent.

Envoi
June 1977

Prince of my blood, the swifts have flown
three times to Africa since then
and for your birthday now return
again. Over the churchyard, they
have been practising all day —
climb and dive, swerve and climb again —
tomorrow's festival flight-pattern.

You murmur in your sleep, as they
in theirs, while I sit polishing
my 'Mirror for a Prince', and say:
This I made for you. Find a space
among the toys in your suitcase
where it can lie, when we take wing
over the ocean to the U. S. A.

See in its warped and spotted glass
one face become another: each,
whatever its profit and loss,
eroded to familiar bone,
my father's, your father's, your own.
Lip-reading here their broken speech,
learn where you stand. Let this be your compass

and talisman. Carry it round
the world, taking your bearings from
its lines. When I was lost, I found
my way by that flickering
dark needle. So may the swift bring
you and your children's children home
to this familiar, well-planted ground.

NOTES

p.15 *Old John Young John.* William Pearse, Rector of Preston Bissett 1735-49.

p.17 *To the Honourable Members of the House of Commons.* Preston Bissett was enclosed in 1782.

p.21 *The Birds o' the Parish.* To lease: to glean, pick up ears of corn.

p.23 *William.* The Old Hat public house was built as a canteen for the builders of the present Church of St John the Baptist in the thirteenth century.

p.24 *To Samuel Greatheed, Evangelist.* 'Samuel Greatheed had entered the [Newport Pagnell] Academy as a student in 1785, having previously served with the Army in the corps of engineers in British North America. From being a student he became a tutor in the college, and after ordination assisted in the ministry of the Word in the newly established cause at Woburn. His military service overseas had given him breadth of vision and deep concern for the unevangelised areas of the world, and when the first soundings for the formation of a missionary society were made Greatheed was one of those who made early response. He journeyed to London on horseback to take part in the proceedings at Baker's Chop House which resulted in the foundation of what later came to be known as the London Missionary Society in 1795, and the despatch in the following year of *The Duff*, the first of the long line of ships to sail under the L.M.S. flag, to the South Seas.'

Rev. R.G. Martin, *The Chapel 1660-1960/The story of the Congregational Church, Newport Pagnell, Bucks*, Newport Pagnell, 1960, pp. 11-12.

p.25 *News from Home.* At the Aylesbury Commission in January 1831, 44 men and boys were found guilty of the charge of destroying paper-making machinery at High Wycomb the previous November. All were transported, some in the *Eliza* and *Proteus* to Van Dieman's Land, others in the *Eleanor* to New South Wales.

p.28 *The Tuscan.* 'On Wednesday, October 16th, Mr. and Mrs. Rodgerson, and Mr. Stallworthy, appointed to the Marquesan Islands, together with Mr. and Mrs. Loxton, appointed to Raiatea, one of the Society Islands, embarked at Gravesend on board the ship *Tuscan*, Captain Stavers, bound for the South Seas.

The Board of Directors gratefully records the sense it enter-
tains of the renewed act of Christian kindness of Alexander
Birnie and Son, Esqrs, owners of the ship *Tuscan*, in presenting
to the Society a free passage for the missionaries and their
wives to the South Sea Islands on board the said ship; also
for the gratuitous freight of supplies for the missionary stations
in that part of the world.'

Evangelical Magazine, 1833, p. 510.

p.29   *The Marquesas*. A group of islands 1,500 miles north-east of
Tahiti.

p.34   *The Beginning. Atua*: god. *Fafa*: mouth. In Marquesan — as in
other Polynesian languages — every vowel is pronounced.

p.35   *The Contest. Marae*: an open space, meeting place. *Tahuata*:
one of the Marquesas Islands.

p.38   *23 August 1844*. The Marquesas were annexed by France in
1842.

p.39   *18 December 1847*. Falealili: a village on the island of Upolu,
Western Samoa.

p.44   *6 November 1859*. 'It was on the morning of Monday, the 7th
inst., that our brother was taken from us. He had gone through
his accustomed Sabbath duties as usual. He preached from the
words, 'Let me die the death of the righteous, and let my last
end be like his.' This subject was no doubt selected with refer-
ence to the death of a native, that had just occurred in Mrs.
Turner's family. It was remarkable, however, in connection
with what was so soon to transpire. His last public service was
the administration of the Lord's Supper, at which he gave an
address from the words, 'I will smite the shepherd, and the
sheep of the flock shall be scattered abroad,' words regarded
by the students of the Institution as of ominous import in the
present weakened state of our Mission. On the previous
Sabbath he had preached from words equally remarkable :
'Come, Lord Jesus; come quickly.' It would seem as if his
mind had been led to those very themes which we may con-
ceive he would have chosen had he known that the coming of
the Lord to him was indeed at hand.'

Letter dated 11 November 1859 from A.W. Murray to the
Rev. Dr. Tidman, the Foreign Secretary of the L.M.S.,
Evangelical Magazine, 1860, p. 284.

78

p.46 *16 December 1859.* Rarotonga: one of the Cook Islands.

p.51 *The Arrival.* Rolling road: a broad track, thirty to forty feet wide, in which every advantage is taken of the natural incline of the land, and from which all trees have been removed, the stumps cut level with the surface, and large holes filled up. The kauri trunks are manhandled along these tracks until they reach the water.
Timber jack: a simple mechanical device for 'jacking up' and rolling kauri logs.
The Circular: a large circular saw.

p.57 *With a copy of Early Northern Wairoa.* A work of local history, *Early Northern Wairoa*, was written by John Stallworthy, formerly M.P. for Kaipara, and printed at the Wairoa Bell & Northern Advertiser Printing Works, Dargaville, 1916.

p.58 *A Couple of Field Postcards / 1919.* 'Another crusade fizzled out after the war. The teetotallers almost succeeded, in 1919, in winning their campaign. Only the votes of the Servicemen overseas, 90 per cent. of whom voted 'wet', saved the New Zealanders from that unlawful thirst which tantalized the Americans in the twenties.'
Keith Sinclair, *A History of New Zealand*, OUP, 1961.

p.59 *Congratulations.* Section: the sections, plots of land, awarded to returning veterans of the Great War were sometimes of poor quality and a cause of subsequent resentment.

p.75 *One for the Road.* Red Devilment / free-falling . . .: the Red Devils are the Parachute Regiment's team of free-fall parachutists.

p.76 'Mirror for a Prince'; *Beowulf* is thought by some to be an early example of the 'Prince's Mirror', a tradition later to include such other works of instruction for young noblemen as Machiavelli's *The Prince* and Castiglione's *The Courtier*.

THE BARE BONES OF THE TREE

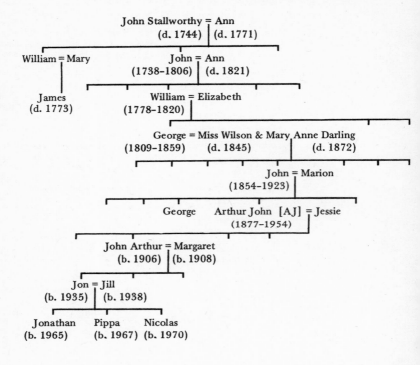

John Stallworthy = Ann
(d. 1744) | (d. 1771)

William = Mary
James
(d. 1773)

John = Ann
(1738–1806) | (d. 1821)

William = Elizabeth
(1778–1820)

George = Miss Wilson & Mary Anne Darling
(1809–1859)   (d. 1845)   (d. 1872)

John = Marion
(1854–1923)

George   Arthur John [AJ] = Jessie
(1877–1954)

John Arthur = Margaret
(b. 1906) | (b. 1908)

Jon = Jill
(b. 1935) | (b. 1938)

Jonathan   Pippa   Nicolas
(b. 1965)   (b. 1967) (b. 1970)